THEODORE ROOSEVELT'S NIGHT RIDE TO THE PRESIDENCY

BY ELOISE CRONIN MURPHY

ADIRONDACK MUSEUM

BLUE MOUNTAIN LAKE, NEW YORK

Unless otherwise indicated, photographs are from the Collection of the Adirondack Museum.

© 1977 by the Adirondack Museum of the
Adirondack Historical Association
Second Printing 1996
All rights reserved
ISBN 0-910020-33-7
Manufactured in the United States of America
Designed by Darrell Hyder, North Brookfield, Massachusetts

FOREWORD.

IN A CENTURY accustomed to instant replay of catastrophic news, it is surprising to learn that only seventy-five years ago an event of importance occurred in the obscurity of the Adirondacks. Somewhere on a muddy stretch of road between Tahawus and Aiden Lair, New York, in the first hours of the morning, Theodore Roosevelt became the twenty-sixth President of the United States. Messages that President William McKinley was failing had reached Roosevelt earlier as he and his party were lunching near Lake Tear-of-the-Clouds on the Marcy trail. Shortly before midnight he began the long, rough ride by buckboard from the Tahawus Club where he was vacationing with his family to the train station at North Creek. When McKinley died at 2:15 a.m., Roosevelt was not aware that the highest office of the land had devolved to him. But Mike Cronin, the third driver of the relay team and the owner and proprietor of Aiden Lair, knew the truth – and kept silent.

Mike Cronin was born January 6, 1861, in Glens Falls, New York, the son of James and Catherine Donovan Cronin. After his graduation from Fort Edward Collegiate Institute, he entered the law office of Judge Enoch Rosencrans, where he studied law until he was afflicted with rheumatism. Advised to go into the north woods, Mike moved to Long Lake to assist the operator of the Sagamore Hotel, Edmund Butler, who became his father-in-law. In 1893 Mike and his wife, Lilian, purchased Aiden Lair, then a log structure, between Newcomb and Minerva. Later they selected a site on higher ground where they erected one of the finest buildings in that vicinity.

Mike and Lilian's daughter, Eloise Cronin (Murphy), grew up with the story of the fateful night her father drove

Teddy Roosevelt to North Creek, establishing a record for speed never broken. From the beginning, newspaper reports contained as much imagination as fact, and time did little to clarify what actually took place before and during that night. In the following account Mrs. Murphy tells the story once again from the point of view of people who had known the Roosevelt family during their frequent visits to Aiden Lair and the Tahawus Club. She draws upon the words and letters of her mother, Lilian Butler Cronin, for the majority of her material. Other letters include those from Mrs. Richard Derby (Ethel Roosevelt), Archibald Roosevelt, Theodore Roosevelt, Jr., Mrs. Adeline Owens Raymond, Norman Hall, Jr., Ervin Angell, and Dr. Harrison I. Braley. Mrs. Murphy has talked extensively to persons of her parent's generation who were eyewitnesses to the event, among them Noah LaCasse, Roosevelt's guide on the Marcy trail, September 13, 1901. And she answers the question, why did Mike Cronin not tell Teddy Roosevelt when he arrived at Aiden Lair at 3:00 a.m., September 14, 1901, that he had been President of the United States for the past three quarters of an hour? Her story is a lively, personal account of a significant moment in the history of the Adirondacks.

Alice Gilborn

Adirondack Museum
Blue Mountain Lake, N.Y.
September, 1976

Map showing Roosevelt's route from the Upper Works, Tahawus Club, to the railroad station in North Creek.

MacNaughton Cottage, Tahawus Club. The Roosevelt family stayed here in 1901.

THEODORE ROOSEVELT'S
NIGHT RIDE
TO THE PRESIDENCY

WHILE WELCOMING CITIZENS at the Pan American Exposition in Buffalo, New York, on September 6, 1901, President William McKinley was shot by Leon Czolgosz, an anarchist terrorist. Vice-President Theodore Roosevelt was notified of this tragedy by Vermont Governor Fisk. At that time the Vice-President was a guest of the Vermont Fish and Game Club on Isle LaMotte, Lake Champlain. He immediately left for the bedside of the President. He arrived in Buffalo Saturday, September 7, 1901. Assured by the surgeon, Dr. Charles Burney, that the President was out of danger, Mr. Roosevelt left by train the following Tuesday, September 10, to join his family vacationing in the Adirondacks.[1] They were guests of James MacNaughton at the Tahawus Club, thirty-five miles north of North Creek, the terminus of the Delaware and Hudson Railroad.[2]

At that time the Tahawus Club controlled the hunting and fishing privileges on 105,000 acres of land belonging to the MacIntyre Iron Works. This tract had never been commercialized for public recreation. It offered unsurpassed opportunity for the Club's sportsmen, who employed from fifteen to twenty guides each season.[3]

My mother, Lilian Butler Cronin, told me, "The Vice-President arrived at the North Creek railroad station September 11, 1901. He was unattended, unannounced – without fanfare. His private secretary, William Loeb, had remained in Albany to be in direct communication with Buffalo.

"At North Creek Mr. Roosevelt picked up a one-seated

President Theodore Roosevelt rowing. The photograph was taken by Arthur Hewitt, with Roosevelt's permission. It appeared in an article entitled "Why the President is so Popular," Ladies Home Journal, *October, 1905.*

buckboard driven by Frank Kelly, operator of a local livery stable, and headed for the Tahawus Club. They stopped for about two hours at Aiden Lair for lunch, while the horses were rested and fed. This was a landmark familiar to Roosevelt since his days as Governor of New York State. With your father, he walked around the porches and spoke of the mountains.[4] Then he spoke about the cactus in the dining room that was blossomed – red, planted in a wooden bucket. Mike sat down and visited with the Vice-President, who had taken his driver right into the dining room at his table. He entertained them with a graphic account of his cougar-hunting expedition in the Rockies the previous year.[5]

"Meanwhile our guests had clamored, 'We must shake

hands with Mr. Roosevelt. We may never have another opportunity. This may be our only chance.' Most of them had had a glimpse of this broad, muscular man, not tall but of solid proportions. He was well set up in flesh, hair greying; as he smiled or talked prominent white teeth flashed beneath his mustache. It was surprising to hear such roaring laughter come from one of so intensely focused expression. He wore pince-nez glasses. Especially marked was his restless vigor.

"Having finished his lunch, the Vice-President came out on the wide veranda facing the Vanderwhacker mountain range, and found about twenty guests and members of the household gathered to meet him. From his previous visits at Aiden Lair, I knew the affable and gregarious character of the man, so I greeted him and said, 'Mr. Roosevelt, will you meet these ladies and gentlemen?' In a most gracious, smiling manner he cordially shook hands with each and chatted enthusiastically concerning his journey through the scenic mountains. Soon, wearing a soft white felt hat and garbed in the customary linen duster of the day, he was back in the buckboard bound for the Tahawus Club."[6]

At the Tahawus-Newcomb road junction, the Vice-President was met by Mrs. Roosevelt. Her carriage was driven that afternoon by Orrin Kellogg, a native of Minerva, and cousin of Secretary of State Frank B. Kellogg, who gave his hand to writing the Kellogg-Briand Peace Pact of 1928. When interviewed on January 4, 1939, Orrin was in his seventy-first year. He had retained a straight, lank frame measuring a full six feet. Well did he represent Adirondack native stock. It was a lesson in classic simplicity as this gentle-mannered neighbor, in moderate measured tones, described that afternoon. "I drove Mrs. Roosevelt to meet him on the main Newcomb highway. He rode the rest of the distance with us. Their son, Theodore, had shot a deer. I remember Mrs. Roosevelt described the incident to her husband."

Of this Theodore Junior wrote, "I remember so well that night in September thirty years ago. I was a young boy at the time, but the excitement of the moment impressed me even though I had just killed my first deer."[7]

"Different times," Orrin said, "I had driven Mrs. Roosevelt down from the Tahawus Club to visit friends at their summer homes, and once out to visit Mrs. Dean Sage of Albany at the Hewitt Lake Club (a mile east of Aiden Lair), where she spent the day. I found Mrs. Roosevelt friendly and sociable. She would chat as we drove along. Mr. Roosevelt spent his time at the Tahawus Club tramping around the woods. His guide was Noah LaCasse."

Before hearing Noah's story, let us learn something of the "Little Roosevelts." How did they "take to the Adirondacks"? The answer came from gracious, friendly Mrs. Adeline Owens Raymond, former postmistress of Minerva, New York, whose keen memory and charming nature made the interview a joy.

"Besides Miss Alice," she said, "who was then a young lady about seventeen, there were Theodore, Jr., Kermit, Archie, Ethel, and Quentin, the baby. I was then employed at the Club. They adapted themselves to the new environment at once. Many guests at the Club called them 'the little Indians.'"

Ethel Roosevelt, now Mrs. Richard Derby, recalled, "We had come up to Tahawus with my mother because my youngest brother, Quentin, had been ill. We were enjoying every minute of the day, its activities so different from those at home. We heard of the attack upon President McKinley with no real understanding of its implications in my case. Then our cup of happiness was full, for my father, ever the most beloved of companions, arrived. We always knew there would be expeditions and adventures."[8]

Archibald Roosevelt wrote of President McKinley's assassination. "I was a small boy at the time and I remember sit-

Theodore Roosevelt, Jr. at Hewitt Lake in the Adirondacks, in 1901.

ting on the piazza one morning and seeing all the old ladies rocking backward and forward. One of them had a newspaper and remarked that Mr. McKinley had been shot in the abdomen. I remember puzzling over this word for quite a while and finally asking what it was. I was much disappointed when I found out that 'abdomen' was nothing but a stomach."[9]

Mrs. Raymond also told of the children's popularity. "They were the liveliest bunch I have ever seen, so full of life and ambition – there was no holding them. On three sides of their camp was a porch. It was nothing to see them as they played 'Chase the Squirrel,' scale the porch posts onto the roof and then come sliding off. The Hudson, just a brook at that point, flows behind the camp. There the children waded, paddled, built dams and, of course, fell in. Wet clothes were always drying on lines strung in nearly every room. They would pick up frogs and snakes, were good to animals. Their father had said, 'Let them go, mother. Let them have some fun.' So off they went, only to be rounded up at meal time when each changed from overalls to a sailor suit. Miss Alice was a beautiful young girl. She was more dignified and precise. She would sleep mornings, and would have breakfast brought to her.

"I must tell you how I happened to wait on the Roosevelts. I was only sixteen years old, had come up to the Club that summer to work for Mrs. Hunter, wife of the superintendent. Her waitresses, older women who had been serving there for years, began to argue among themselves over who would have the Roosevelt table, who would wait on the Vice-President and his family. Well, to settle the argument, didn't Mrs. Hunter put me, just a kid who had never waited on table in my life, in the dining room to take care of the Roosevelt family! They were wonderful to me, knew I was a greenhorn and helped all they could to make it easier for me. I enjoyed the assignment.

"Guests of the Club were served in the main dining room. The MacNaughtons and the Mastens gave up their tables to the Roosevelts, and went to transient tables themselves. To make it easy for me, Mrs. Young, the governess, used to decide what they were to eat because the youngsters didn't listen long enough to know what to order. Their mother or the governess would send them from the table if they didn't behave.

"Let me tell you, the Roosevelts made it an exciting event with their stories of Adirondack adventure. The usual formality of the Club dining room entirely disappeared, for Mr. Roosevelt himself kept the conversation buzzing. There were no 'airs' about the man, and he seemed to love to talk. He would talk to everyone – from one table to another. Even while telling a joke he'd have a serious expression. There were no airs about Mrs. Roosevelt either. She showed an interest in us all, would ask all kinds of questions about how we managed. I remember that she marveled when she heard how one of the mothers in Newcomb managed her many children alone while her husband was working up at the Club all summer. She was a dainty, pretty woman, having dark hair and a smooth skin. While at the Club she wore one of those khaki short brown skirts. I had forgotten her features until I saw the oil painting which hangs in one of the corridors of the White House in Washington. There she looks just as I saw her in the Club in 1901."

Canadian-born Noah LaCasse had previously guided Roosevelt when, as Governor of New York State, he was a guest of Robert C. Pruyn's camp Santanoni, on Newcomb Lake.[10] To consult Noah I drove twelve miles up the Roosevelt–Marcy Highway to Newcomb, there to meet the man who had been "camping and tramping with Roosevelt." A September gale blew ominously, as massive clouds dimmed the sunset. Five

Roosevelt's guide, Noah LaCasse.

miles – past the Roosevelt monument; seven miles – past the turn which Roosevelt took for Tahawus; nine miles – through the clearing from which can be seen the whole Marcy range, with Marcy itself boldly challenging the advancing storm. West of Lake Harris I found Noah LaCasse's plain, white clapboard house and the man himself, Theodore Roosevelt's choice, the "picked guide." Of independent mind, Noah looked at me, clutched my hand firmly, and spoke distinctly. Honest, cheerful, likeable, a conservationist, he deserved the trust of Theodore Roosevelt.

Noah came to Newcomb from Canada when he was seventeen. Again and again since 1901 he had related his story to news reporters, historians, novelists, neighbors and strangers. He was never a weary or mechanical teller. At seventy-five he still recalled with enthusiasm and pride the events of the two days at Tahawus that proved to be most memorable in his long life as an Adirondack woodsman. Choosing his words cautiously, just as he would pick up a trail in the woods, and in slightly accented tones, he recounted:

"When Orrin Kellogg brought the Roosevelts into Tahawus Club the evening of September 11th, I was there.

"'Hello, Noah!' the Vice-President called.

"Hello, Teddy,' I hailed him. When I guided him up at Pruyn's Santanoni, he had instructed me: 'Everyone calls me Teddy. I understand it very well. Call me Teddy.'

"'You going with us?' he asked immediately.

"'I will let you know in a minute,' I replied. I asked a party I was guiding if I could go with Mr. Roosevelt. 'Yes, by all means, go,' they said. So I reported that I would be with him directly.

"The son, Theodore, spent his time hunting with another guide, John Hall. However, Mr. Roosevelt wanted to go mountain climbing with me. Ed Dimick was to guide Mrs. Roosevelt and the children. On September 12th we all hiked to Lake Colden and camped overnight."

Of this expedition, Mrs. Derby wrote, "I think it rained which made us feel really hardened woodsmen. There was a delicious supper, and the camp fire and the stories. Next morning my father started up to Mt. Marcy and we went back to the Club."[11]

"When morning came," said Noah, "it was arranged that Dimick would take Mrs. Roosevelt and the children back to the MacNaughton camp when the rain let up. The rest of us – Mr. Roosevelt, James MacNaughton, the two Robinson boys (guests of the Club who had come along) and I – left to go to Mt. Marcy. The trail was slippery and muddy. Going was bad. Mr. Roosevelt carried a pack basket for about three miles. He had said, 'Let me carry your pack basket. I never had one of those on my back in my life.' We went to the top of the mountain, walking in rain and clouds so thick we could not see ten feet ahead of us.

"'How can you find your way here?' he asked.

"'Well, I've been up here a few times before.' Then I showed him piers of stones from which we guides make our sights.

"From the mountain top we could see only a few feet around. We were right in the clouds, then it suddenly cleared for about ten minutes. The sun came out – could see a long distance. Mr. Roosevelt looked the whole country over, asked questions about the different bodies of water that could be seen.[12]

"'Beautiful country, beautiful country!' he said over and over. The sky darkened, heavy clouds settling like a sea stretching out below us."

Beyond the timber line, above the clouds warmed by the sun, Mt. Marcy – Tahawus, the Cloud Splitter.[13] It was a fitting threshold for the presidential career of the great conservationist Theodore Roosevelt.[14] There on the highest point in the Empire State stood the man destined for the highest position in the nation.

"Unknown to Roosevelt," Lilian Cronin related, "at eight o'clock that morning [September 13, 1901] William Loeb, his private secretary, had come into North Creek with a special train to carry the Vice-President to Buffalo. It had become apparent that there was only the slimmest chance that President McKinley would survive. The Cabinet members decided to summon the Vice-President with the following message which Loeb telephoned Friday morning, September 13th, to Michael Breen [in charge of the Lower Works] at the Lower Club House, termination of the telephone line:

```
                              Buffalo, N.Y.
Hon. T. Roosevelt

The President appears to be dying and
members of Cabinet in Buffalo think you
should lose no time in coming.

                         Elihu Root
```

"Breen sent this message by wagon to David Hunter, superintendent of the Tahawus Club. He chose guide Harrison Hall to deliver it up the Marcy trail to the Vice-President.[15] Mr. Loeb spent most of the next twenty hours in a state of frustration. He kept calling your father [Mike Cronin] at Aiden Lair. It was past mid-day when he learned that Roosevelt was on Mt. Marcy. He had already started arrangements for relays of drivers to bring the Vice-President to North Creek."

Mr. Lee Waddell, brother of Assemblyman William Waddell and a handsome and prosperous North Creek businessman, described that tedious day at North Creek. "I was there all day with Loeb waiting for the President's arrival. There were no other officials with Loeb. We visited, walked about. It was mighty tiresome, but he wouldn't go farther than the American Hotel which is in sight of the station. There was a small gathering of villagers. News didn't fly in those days as now. Wouldn't even know about it on the outskirts at that time. I mean even up as far as North River [a hamlet five miles up the Hudson]."

Noah LaCasse, continuing his story, said: "We came down the mountain for our lunch at Lake Tear-of-the-Clouds where our packs had been left. No lean-to or fireplace was there at that time. Anyhow, it was too wet to build a fire. We sat in the grass just a few feet from the source of the Hudson River, Lake Tear-of-the-Clouds. It is a bit of water about five hundred feet long and not over five feet deep. Fed by springs, the water is cold – quite clear. Balsam trees border one end. The rest is surrounded by a grassy clearing. A good size flat rock sticks out of the water directly in front of where we were sitting.

"There was a can of ox tongue to be opened. 'Noah, have you got a knife?' asked Mr. Roosevelt. Before I could answer he said, 'Oh, what a fool I am to ask a guide if he's got a knife!' He opened the can himself saying, 'Noah's the one to be waited on first. He's been doing all the work.' Roosevelt was a real sportsman.

"We saw a man coming up the trail through the fog. It was Harrison Hall. Mr. Roosevelt squinted. You know he was near-sighted. 'Do you mean to say that's Harrison Hall?' he asked. I said, 'Yes, Sir.' I could tell Harrison Hall by his gait. He came up and handed Mr. Roosevelt a paper."

"What happened next angered my grandfather, Harrison Hall," Norman Hall of Minerva told me. "He had hurried as fast as the wet, slippery, foggy trail would permit any guide to travel. He knew the message he bore was urgent, and he had not even taken time to tell Mrs. Roosevelt about it when they met on the trail below. The Vice-President took the message, read it, said nothing but calmly turned and finished his lunch. My grandfather never had much to say about that moment. It left him flabbergasted."

Artist's conjectural depiction of Roosevelt receiving the message telling of McKinley's failing health, illustrated in T. R., A Typical American. *The Vice-President was not hunting on this trip. (The Theodore Roosevelt Collection, Harvard College Library, Cambridge, Massachusetts.)*

When they reached the Upper Works that evening, Beverley Robinson, one of the party, entered in the Register of the Adirondack Club: "... At 2:00 o'clock were lunching ... near Lake Tear, when Harrison Hall, guide, appeared with the first dispatches. He had come through from the Club House, around the Flowed Lands, over a wretched trail, in three hours and ten minutes. Col. Roosevelt reached the Upper Works at 5:15."

Years later to a friend, Theodore Roosevelt remarked, "There wasn't a thought in my mind but that the President would live and I was perfectly happy until I saw the runner come out on the trail some distance away. I had had a bully tramp and was looking forward to dinner with the interest only an appetite worked up in the woods gives you. When I saw the runner I instinctively knew he had bad news – the worst news in the world."[16]

"Finally," Noah recalled, "Mr. Roosevelt said, 'Complicated, complicated, but I don't want to become President through a graveyard. I would rather work for it.'"[17]

"We walked the twelve miles in three hours and a quarter," said Noah, "back to the Club about five-thirty. We made preparations for the family to leave the next day. I was washing Mr. Roosevelt's muddy pants and shoes in the river, ready to pack up for home when he received another message, the forepart of the evening, about President McKinley failing. Then about ten o'clock he received a message that McKinley was dying, so he made preparations to start at once."[18]

"Four and a half hours had elapsed before Mr. Roosevelt received definite word that the President was dying," said Lilian Cronin. "Tension all over the country was increasing, not only because of the President's approaching death, but because exact information concerning Theodore Roosevelt's movements could not be determined. Why did he not leave for Buffalo as soon as he came down from Mt. Marcy? Why did he wait until news came that McKinley was actually dying? Perhaps he had in mind the ruthless criticisms of political enemies who deliberately misinterpreted his sympathy and concern when only the week before he had hurried from Isle LaMotte on Lake Champlain, Vermont, to the bedside of the wounded President. These commentators had insinuated that the Vice-President's concern was for quite selfish reasons."

At any rate, years later when addressing a group of school children at the Roosevelt home in New York City, on the seventy-fifth anniversary of her husband's birth, Mrs. Roosevelt said:

"When the party came down from Mt. Marcy, my husband came to me and he said, 'I'm not going unless I am really needed. I have been there once and that shows how I feel. But I will not go to stand beside those people who are suffering and anxious. I'm going to wait here.' That was all very well, but the President was taken so ill that in the night they came and knocked at my door and they said it was absolutely imperative that my husband leave at once. He took a most terrific ride in the middle of the night."

"I served Mr. Roosevelt a light lunch," recalled Mrs. Raymond, "while they were getting the horse and wagon ready for the first relay. No, he didn't seem too upset, although I remember how he rushed through the meal. Mrs. Roosevelt was not one to get confused or upset either. I remember everyone remarking how calm she was."

"Father and mother," related Mrs. Derby, "as always were calm and quiet in the presence of an emergency, but I well remember that we children knew and understood something of the import of the news."[19]

Mrs. Raymond continued, "One of the youngsters cried and took on because the father was leaving. The child knew that President McKinley had been shot and was afraid if their father became President, he'd be shot too. At just ten-thirty, Theodore Roosevelt left us. He rode away with David Hunter in a wagon drawn by a big, bay horse."

Club guide Ira Proctor witnessed the departure. "I've always been amused at what the newspapers said about the breakneck speed of the ride from the Tahawus Upper Club," he told me. "It was Jimmy Lindsay's big bay – must have weighed over 1400 pounds. Of course he didn't poke along any, but he hardly broke a record."

Of this episode David Hunter said: "They [the Roosevelt party] returned to the Upper Works in the late afternoon. Teddy did not seem to be the least bit exhausted. He ate a good supper. Sometime after supper I hitched up a horse that had been skidding logs all day, harnessed him to a light wagon [buckboard] and tied a lantern on the rear axle. You remember that ride used to be the ten miles from the Lower Works to the Upper Works, full of mud holes and corduroy. ... It had been raining a lot during the last few days and the road was in terrible shape. So we started out down through the mud – plunk, plunk, plunk."

The first ten miles completed, Orrin Kellogg drove Mr. Roosevelt the next nine miles to Aiden Lair. Of this second relay Orrin said:

"My horses had traveled twenty-five miles already that day. I drove them in from North Creek where I had taken Club members to the train. On returning I was stopped at the Tahawus Post Office at the Lower Club House and told to have the horses rested for the second relay. That was about one or two o'clock in the afternoon. Different ones coming down from the Upper Club stopped to be sure I had the team ready. As Hunter came down in the one-seater wagon with Mr. Roosevelt, we could see his lantern light up at the Gallager place about two miles away. That was my signal to hitch up the bays. Mr. Roosevelt stopped just long enough to use the telephone and drink a cup of coffee. This took not over ten minutes. I was driving a two-seater. Mr. Roosevelt got in the back, had just a bag which he carried right in the seat with him. It was raining, kind of a drizzle. The road was quite muddy. Here is my old raincoat which Mr. Roosevelt used to protect him from the mud splashing from the wheels."[20]

"He talked but little – asked what the lights were when we came to Kay's place. There was a dance there that night and the crowd hadn't all gone home yet. We talked some about McKinley being shot. I remember him saying: 'I think if it had been I who had been shot, he [the assassin] wouldn't have got away so easily. I think I'd have guzzled him first. I'm waiting for a message from Elihu Root, the Secretary of War. Mr. Root said, 'The President seems to be dying.' Billy Loeb said, when I talked to him on the telephone at the Tahawus Post Office, that the President *was* dying.'

"Mr. Roosevelt was a very plain man – he was plain spoken. He wasn't any afraid. You could drive as fast as you'd a mind to and nothing scared him a bit."

This second relay had been expected to reach Aiden Lair at about two o'clock in the morning.

"Everyone was straining his eyes to catch first sight of the travelers," recalled Lilian Cronin. "When Mr. Loeb phoned Mike from North Creek that President McKinley had died at 2:15 a.m., the tension heightened. Each hoped to be the first to see the new President of the United States, and each had been asked by Mike not to mention the fateful news to the distinguished person expected at any moment. A Dr. Moore of White Plains, New York, who had come down from Nathan's camp on Balfour Lake to join us, had approached your father and declared, 'Mike, I'll give you fifty dollars if you'll let me drive the President to North Creek.' But mindful of the message he had received, your father was in no humor to let a novice drive the new President over the mountain road on such a night. Again and again, Mr. Loeb telephoned only to be told, 'Not yet, no sign of them yet!'"

Mike Cronin reported: "I received notice just about noon, over the telephone, to have everything ready for quick work. That is just exactly what I did and I was soon ready to start at any moment that Mr. Roosevelt might reach Aiden Lair. I had a span of blacks, Frank and Dick, fast steppers, hooked up. What was still better than their speed, they knew the road as well as I did myself, having made the trip from three to six times a week all summer. I had expected Mr. Roosevelt along several hours sooner. While I was watching for him I was fooled several times. There was a dance at William Kay's house, three miles above my place, and after midnight the crowd was driving home. I kept thinking that each one was Mr. Roosevelt. There was a rainy mist or a misty rain and this made the night, already very dark, perfectly black."

"At last, at three o'clock that morning, steady, dependable

Morgan horses Frank and Dick and their driver, Mike Cronin. This picture appeared in The New York Herald, *Sunday, September 22, 1901, days after Roosevelt's famous ride.*

Orrin Kellogg pulled up his horses beside the wooden platform landing at Aiden Lair," said Lilian Cronin. "The President of the United States stepped out. There was no demonstration. Only necessary words were spoken, and those in quiet tones, as Theodore Roosevelt climbed into your father's waiting carriage.

"As the carriage was about to pull away from Aiden Lair someone raised the question of where to put the lantern. It was suggested that it be put on the dashboard but Mike said it would only be a bother. Finally Roosevelt said, 'Here, give it to me!' and settled the matter. Then they started, over sixteen miles of winding mountain road, to the special train at North Creek."

"I had expected Mr. Roosevelt along several hours sooner," continued Mike Cronin, "as he might have been had it not been for the careless bungling in getting word to him. He ought to have been hustled along faster too.... Mr. Roosevelt is one of the nerviest men I ever saw and I am not easily scared myself. At one place, while we were going down a slippery hill, one of the horses stumbled. It was a ticklish bit of road and I was beginning to get somewhat uneasy and began holding the team back, but Mr. Roosevelt said, 'Oh, that doesn't matter. Push ahead!'"[21]

"At another time we were going around a curve on a dugout which, you know, is a piece of road cut in a steep hillside. It was a dangerous place, for if we had been upset we would have been pitched headlong down seventy-five or a hundred feet. I told Mr. Roosevelt of the danger as we drew near the risky spot and suggested that I slow up until we struck better road. He replied, 'Not at all. If you are not afraid I am not.

A bridge into North Creek in 1906. (Courtesy of Eloise Cronin Murphy.)

Push ahead!' And so we did. Luckily, we had a clear road and did not meet a single team through the whole drive.

"Did the President talk much? Very little about the situation. Most of the time he seemed to be in deep thought and very sad. About all the words he spoke were, 'Keep up the pace!' He held his watch in his hand all the while and kept continually asking how far we still had to go.... I shall not drive over that dark road again without seeming to hear him say, 'Push along! Hurry up! Go faster!'

"I made the last sixteen mile relay in one hour and forty-one minutes. It was the darkest night I ever saw. I could not even see my horses except for the spots where the flickering lantern light fell on them. This time beat the best record ever made before by a quarter of an hour, and that record I had made myself with a two-seater in daylight."

When they arrived at the long, flat stretch of road by the Bibbey farm about two miles from North Creek, Mr. Roosevelt again asked the distance ahead and decided they should halt. He got out, took a few brisk steps, straightened his tie and smoothed his suit for, as he reminded my father, there might be some notables, no telling who, to be met at the station. To Mike Cronin this was a treasured pause, as he watched his friend the President of the United States "spruce up" for the occasion. Besides, those fleeting moments gave the horses the chance they needed "to blow" before the last dash.[22]

Dawn was breaking as the ride ended at North Creek.[23] "There was the thunder of the horses' hoofs as they clattered over the planks of the bridge which spanned the Hudson," recalled Reverend A. D. Angell, pastor of the North Creek Methodist Church, who was waiting at the station.[24]

"It was just coming daylight," said Lee Waddell. "Mr. Loeb and I sat on the steps right by the scales of the old railroad station. 'There comes Mike Cronin now!' I said to Loeb. Then they came flying down Main Street."

"I heard them coming," put in Mrs. Cora Montgomery Alexander, owner of a millinery and gift shop at North Creek. "I got up out of bed and ran to the window. How fast were they going? Just as fast as they could travel!"

"As they swung into the station," resumed Mr. Waddell, "President Roosevelt jumped out of the wagon, greeting us both."

Mr. Loeb's long wait was over and only then did President Roosevelt learn of McKinley's death, as his secretary handed him this telegram:

```
              Buffalo, N.Y., Sept. 14, 1901

Hon. Theodore Roosevelt
North Creek, New York

The President died at 2:15 this morning.

              John Hay
              Secretary of State
```

To Mike Cronin there was nothing singular nor presumptuous in the fact that he had driven sixteen miles with the President of the United States without telling him William McKinley had died. His reason, in Mike's own words was, "I did not want to add to Mr. Roosevelt's anxiety."

Lee Waddell observed, "When Mr. Roosevelt got out of the wagon, he was swift, no sign of fatigue. He turned and rushed up the platform steps two at a time — just as I've seen him dart up the State Capitol steps when he was Governor — like a sparrow. There was no delay."

Dr. Harrison I. Braley of North Creek wrote: "As a boy of nine I had the privilege and thrill of witnessing one of the highlights of our town's history — the boarding of the train by Theodore Roosevelt the night he became President of the United States. Naturally, the three Alfred R. Braley sons —

Telegram dispatched from Roosevelt from Ballston Spa, to Mrs. Roosevelt telling her of President McKinley's death. The message was posted in the guest Register of the Adirondack Club, now at the Adirondack Museum.

New York Herald article, September 22, 1901, describing Roosevelt's wild ride from Tahawus to North Creek. The event was reported throughout the world.

Reese, eleven; myself, Harrison, nine; and Downing, eight – begged our father to let us go to the station. Father at first objected as it was a long walk on a rainy night with no lights other than oil lanterns. He finally consented and took us late in the evening. There were of course a great many local and nearby adults and a small sprinkling of children. The night being wet and chilly, some of us took shelter in the warm station rather than remain on the platform after the switching of the special train on which steam was maintained all night. As father expected, Downing and I fell asleep in the warm room while Reese remained outside with father most of the night. The next thing Downing and I realized was our father shaking us awake and saying, 'I thought you wanted to see the President. You will have to hurry.' We bolted out of the station door just in time to see the President hurry across the platform, hurry up the steps of his special car, turn quickly, wave to the crowd, and hurry inside. By the time the President was through the door the train was under motion, and as boys will, we, with others, rushed down the tracks until the train disappeared. We were then hurried home, and dawn was breaking by the time we were in bed. Of course these events were of such unusual character that a boy of nine could never forget."[25]

That afternoon in Buffalo, Theodore Roosevelt took the oath of office, becoming the twenty-sixth President of the United States.

Railroad station in North Creek, 1888. The station was recently placed on the National Register of Historic Places.

The moment Theodore Roosevelt's train pulled out of North Creek station, Mike Cronin went to the nearest telephone. He called his wife, Lilian, who was waiting anxiously at Aiden Lair. "We made it in one hour and forty-one minutes. Yes, yes, we're all right. The President just left."

"The famous ride was over," said Lilian Cronin. "Secretary Loeb's long wait was over and President Roosevelt learned of President McKinley's death, which your father had not disclosed because he thought it the proper thing for the announcement to be made where the oath of office could be administered, especially did he wish to save President Roosevelt added anxiety on the weary journey.

"Never again did Theodore Roosevelt visit this section of the North Country, but he always kept in touch with your father by letter, by message and by interview."

The record set by the span of Morgans from Aiden Lair to North Creek was never equalled. For years afterward various sportsmen and "lumber kings" strove to beat their time, but the record stands to this day. Traveling over hard roads in swift cars nowadays, it is hard to appreciate what they did. To do so, keep in mind it was a black night. A continuous three days' rain had turned the thirty-five mile crooked, mountainous, in many places, corduroy, dirt road into a "mud track." It had become muddier each hour. Frank and Dick ran not only the longest but the last, and therefore the muddiest, stretch, the "home stretch." A comparison of the time and distance involved in each relay still gives one some idea of their feat. Following is a summary:

RELAY	DRIVER	ROUTE	MILES	TIME
1st	Hunter	Tahawus Club to Tahawus Post Office	10	2 hrs.
2nd	Kellogg	Tahawus Post Office to Aiden Lair	9	2 hrs. 20 mins.
3rd	Cronin	Aiden Lair to North Creek	16	1 hr. 41 mins.

Surrey on display at the Adirondack Museum may be one of the three horsedrawn vehicles that carried Roosevelt on his ride to the presidency. (Gift of the family of Michael F. Cronin.)

"At first glance the Morgans seemed an odd pair," said Lilian Cronin. "Dick, a long-legged eight year old, weighed about 1,000 pounds. He was tall, awkward, more than twice Frank's age, but he was a smart leader. As I recall, when your father bought Dick he was told the horse had raced at the Pottersville Fairs. Frank, the four year old, referred to as "the colt," was shorter and weighed about the same. Your grandfather [James Cronin] had raised and trained the colt in Glens Falls. Dick's age and experience with Frank's youth and spirit proved the right combination for their part in Theodore Roosevelt's night ride to the Presidency."

Having charted what the beasts, the Morgans, accomplished, let us examine the accomplishment of the man, Adirondack guide Harrison Hall. Keep in mind he was fifty-three years old. "At age seventy-five my grandfather could carry a buck on his shoulders," said Norman Hall, Jr. Harrison Hall was climbing most of the time on his nine-mile journey from Tahawus Club to Lake Tear-of-the-Clouds. It was raining, the trail was wet, slippery, and therefore dangerous.

In conclusion, a word should be said about the Morgans' shoes. Would they not be unusual souvenirs? Made of steel, skillfully shaped to fit the hoofs of only Frank and Dick! There was talk of persons possessing these historic horseshoes, even Alice Roosevelt who allegedly was given the last one when she visited Aiden Lair some years later. Their fate, in fact, was simple. My mother said, "No one ever gave the horseshoes a thought; no one kept track of them and they probably were kicked off in the pasture or along the road somewhere. One thing is certain. Your father never sold them to anyone. If he had kept track of the horseshoes, he would have given them to the first person who asked for them. However, your father liked a good story and I wouldn't be surprised if he had a hand in starting this one."

While at Aiden Lair the winter of 1939 I composed the following lines about these events:

> The horseshoes worn by the rangy blacks
> Have long been lost
> And gone are their tracks,
> But oft' on a rainy September night
> There's thudding of hoofs
> Of horses in flight,
> As out from Tahawus on his famous night ride
> Comes Theodore Roosevelt
> This nation to guide!

FOOTNOTES.

1. Margaret Leech, *In the Days of McKinley* (New York: Harper and Brothers, 1959), p. 599.
2. James MacNaughton was a direct descendant of the MacIntyre family, whose efforts to mine the extensive iron deposits in that area in the early 1800s proved too costly. That mine is now owned and operated by NL Industries, Inc. It has one of the largest titanium deposits in the world.
3. Arthur H. Masten, *The Story of Adirondac* (Syracuse, N.Y.: Adirondack Museum/Syracuse University Press, 1968), p. 189. See also, Harold K. Hochschild, *The MacIntyre Mine — From Failure to Fortune* (Blue Mountain Lake, N.Y.: The Adirondack Museum, 1962).
4. According to Mrs. Teresa Cronin Maier, the Cronin children and their playmates used to say, "If we go around the porches twenty times we've traveled a mile."
5. Later Mr. Roosevelt's article describing the hunt appeared in *Scribner's Magazine*. See Theodore Roosevelt, "With the Cougar Hounds," *Scribner's Magazine* (October-November, 1901).
6. Abner Parker, of Newcomb, who several times drove Roosevelt when Governor up to Santanoni, and Claude Gallager, who as a ten year old saw Roosevelt go by his farm en route to Tahawus said, "He always wore a big white felt brimmed hat."
7. Letter to the author, August 1, 1939. Also entered in the "Register, Adirondack Club" (1878-1921), September 4, 1901. Collection of the Adirondack Museum.
8. Letter to the author, June 5, 1958.
9. Letter to the author, August 25, 1958.
10. Santanoni, twelve miles above Aiden Lair, is an estate of 12,550 acres which in 1974 became the property of the State of New York.
11. Letter to the author, June 5, 1958.
12. They are, for the most part, Lake Placid and parts of Lake Champlain. On a clear day one can see the spires of Montreal, eighty miles to the north.
13. Marcy, elevation 5,344 feet, was named by state geologist Ebenezer Emmons on August 5, 1837, in honor of New York gov-

ernor William Learned Marcy. One month later, in September 1837, poet and author Charles Fenno Hoffman visited the peak and dubbed it "Tahawus," an Indian word meaning "cloud splitter." Contrary to local legend, Hoffman, not the Indians, gave the mountain its poetic epithet. See Russell M. L. Carson, *Peaks and People of the Adirondacks* (Glens Falls, N.Y.: The Adirondack Mountain Club, 1973), 57.

14. Theodore Roosevelt's significant contribution to the cause of conservation is acknowledged by contemporary historians. See, for example: Samuel E. Morison et al., *Growth of the American Republic*, 2 vols, 6th ed., (New York: The Oxford University Press, 1969), 2: 307-309; R. Hofstadter et al., *The United States: The History of a Republic*, 2nd ed., (Englewood Cliffs, N.J.: Prentice-Hall, 1967), 656.

15. There has been some confusion over what messages were actually delivered by Harrison Hall to Vice-President Roosevelt on the Marcy trail. It appears likely that Hall was carrying the following message from William Loeb, Jr., who was by then waiting at North Creek: "Cortelyou [George B. Cortelyou, Secretary to President McKinley] wires President's condition causes gravest apprehension. Ansley Wilcox telephoned 6:00 a.m. slight improvement. Advise your coming here immediately. Will meet you if necessary. Will send special engine to bring you in case you miss the 10:20 train [from North Creek] this morning." The message sent by Secretary of War, Elihu Root, may not have reached Roosevelt until after his return to the Upper Works in the early evening. See note 18.

16. John J. Leary, Jr., *Talks with T. R.* (New York: Houghton Mifflin, Co., 1920).

17. Accounts of what Roosevelt actually said upon reading the message handed to him by Harrison Hall do not all agree. The *New York Herald*, Sunday, September 22, 1901, reported that Roosevelt simply stated, "Gentlemen, I must return to the club house at once." Hugh R. Paine in his article, "I Always Called Him 'Ted'," *The New York Masonic Outlook* (December, 1938), quoted Noah LaCasse as telling him Roosevelt's response was, "'Complicated, complicated!' That was all he said." In 1948, LaCasse wrote Edward A. Harmes about the event and reported Roosevelt's statement as "Complicated, complicated, complicated. Let's pack up and go." In his article, "2:15 A.M.: T.R.'s Ride from Tahawus to North Creek," *The Adirondac*, XXVII (November-December, 1963), 88-92, Harmes recorded Roosevelt's words as "Complicated, complicated, complicated. I must

return to the Club at once." David H. Beetle, "The Man Who Climbed Mt. Marcy," *Utica Post Dispatch*, March 5, 1950, said that LaCasse once asked Roosevelt, "'Would you like to be President?' 'Not by way of the graveyard,' said Teddy." It is probable that Noah LaCasse was recalling Roosevelt's response on two separate occasions when Mrs. Murphy interviewed him.

18. The message that McKinley was failing may have been Root's telegram, "The President appears to be dying ...." The last message Roosevelt received was from Cortelyou posted from Buffalo at 9:00 p.m., September 13, 1901. It read simply, "The President is dying." See note 15.

19. Letter to the author, June 5, 1958.

20. Orrin Kellogg gave this raincoat to the author. It was a gift to him from one of the Club members.

21. Words spoken by Mike Cronin on the telephone to a newspaper reporter. The story appeared the next day in *The New York Herald*, Sunday, September 15, 1901.

22. Incident of the sixteen mile journey Mike Cronin related to his wife, Lilian. He never told it to anyone else.

23. There are a number of discrepancies in contemporary accounts concerning the exact time of Roosevelt's departure from the Tahawus Club and his arrival and departure from North Creek.

24. Letter to the author, August 22, 1958, from Ervin Angell, son of Reverend Angell.

25. Letter to the author, July 9, 1958.

26. Recorded by Beverley R. Robinson in the "Register – Adirondack Club" (1878-1921). Club name later in that period was changed to Tahawus Club.